Words of praise for *The Views From Mo...*

FROM REEVE LINDBERGH:

"Marjorie Ryerson is an award-winning poet, photographer, journalist and teacher. Her new book of poetry, *The Views from Mount Hunger*, is a delight. Ryerson has a profound, intuitive understanding of the natural world, and she casts a sly glance at human behavior even at its most absurd. Music and musicians appear throughout: a touching glimpse of Van Cliburn's awkwardness at the piano just before he plays Rachmaninoff, several tributes to Mahler that evoke barn swallows, tides, winds, mist, and light. Fellow poets are here, in a nod to Wallace Stevens, a poem for Coleman Barks, and another in the form of a letter to Anne Sexton. There are poems about family members, poems about love, and one, beautifully, is just about cows. *The Views from Mount Hunger* is a collection no thoughtful reader should miss."

Reeve Lindbergh, daughter of aviator-writers Charles A. and Anne Morrow Lindbergh, is the author of more than two dozen rhyming books for children and other books for adults, including *Under a Wing: a Memoir*; *No More Words: A Journal Of My Mother, Anne Morrow Lindbergh*; *Forward From Here: Leaving Middle Age and Other Unexpected Adventures*; and *Two Lives*. Her work has appeared in a number of periodicals and magazines, including the *New York Times Book Review*, *The New Yorker* and *The Washington Post*. She lives in Barnet, Vermont, with her husband, writer Nat Tripp, and an assortment of animals, enjoying visits from their children and grandchildren.

FROM ARCHER MAYOR:

"Marjorie Ryerson's poems skip past my usual analytical frontal lobe to be absorbed among my quirkier notions. They bounce around and interact where I store my spontaneous one-liners, my occasional zingers, my skeptical observations, and my sentimental, tearful soul. Her clarity of language, her sharp eye for detail, her simple eloquence, and, sometimes, wonderful humor reflect the tangled thoughts of so many of us in a confusing, often hurtful world. Only she says it better than we can. She turns on the light in places in need of it, and gives us the means to see."

Archer Mayor, throughout his life, has at least tried to assuage his demons using creativity and public service. In pursuit of the first, he has written two history books and 33 novels. Practicing the second, among other things, he has been a firefighter/EMT, a police officer, and is currently a death investigator for Vermont's Office of the Chief Medical Examiner.

Words of praise for *The Views From Mount Hunger*

FROM CHARD DeNIORD:

"Marjorie Ryerson observes the natural world with bold scrutiny in *The Views From Mount Hunger*, reminding her reader by reminding herself first that "poems are the scraping away of the surfaces / to get at what is underneath. The last-gas-before-desert hope for us." In overhearing herself in her candid musings, she acknowledges that "words clarify" but also "deceive." Yet, she is willing to write in this space between, risking deception for the sake of capturing her "wonder." She writes with this courage, finding one reason after another to celebrate her experience of being alive with plain spoken exuberance and instructions on how to do the same. As a bold, unabashed witness to mortal consciousness, she reminds her readers with a manifold array of literal and figurative examples that "this present moment is all that we have.""

Chard deNiord is the author of seven books of poetry, most recently *In My Unknowing* and *Interstate*. He is also the author of two books of interviews with eminent American poets titled *Sad Friends, Drowned Lovers, Stapled Songs* and *I Would Lie to You If I Could*. He served as Poet Laureate of Vermont from 2015 to 2019 and taught at Providence College for 22 years, where he is Professor Emeritus of English and Creative writing.

FROM SYDNEY LEA:

"In *The Views from Mount Hunger,* Marjorie Ryerson asserts that "We have a choice / between types of darkness: / the darkness that obscures / or the darkness of inner peace." The author knows both kinds, but with a hunger befitting her title, she seeks and finds affirmation, often by recourse to music (the many musical suites here are deft and distinctive) and sometimes simply by keen observation, and always by way of selfless love. In the end, Ms. Ryerson leaves us with that too rare commodity: hope."

Sydney Lea (www.sydneylea.net) is the 2021 recipient of Vermont's Governor's Award for Excellence in the Arts. A former Pulitzer finalist and winner of the 1998 Poets' Prize, he was Vermont's Poet Laureate from 2011 to 2015. He is the author of 23 books and the recipient of fellowships from the Guggenheim, Rockefeller and Fulbright Foundations. For many years, he taught at Dartmouth, Yale, Middlebury, and Wesleyan Colleges and served on the faculty of the MFA in Writing program at the Vermont College of Fine Arts. Lea has also served as a visiting professor at numerous colleges in Europe. His work has appeared in all the major literary journals, and more than sixty anthologies. He has long been active in conservation. In 2012, he was named a Hero of Conservation by Field & Stream magazine. He is married, and has five children and seven grandchildren. He lives in Newbury, Vermont.

Words of praise for *The Views From Mount Hunger*

FROM SCUDDER PARKER:

> *The river sucks my body toward it*
> *with each paddle stroke. It owns me.*
> *And each time I stop to swim—to wash*
> *the ovens of the Mississippi summer*
> *from my body—I shed my single layer*
> *of clothes and slip over the gunnels*
> *into the fierce grip of something*
> *more than river.*

"...writes Marjorie Ryerson in "Leaving Myself Behind," one of the many startling, powerful poems in her collection, *The Views from Mount Hunger*. Marjorie plunges in, writing from inside the wildness of the river, one hand on the canoe (we hope) but unafraid of the tug and swirl that surrounds her. It may be her childhood where her mother rises up from the dining room table and announces "I am going to the ocean," and the family sits frozen in response—again. It may be in her lovely, intimate tribute "To Anne Sexton" or in her passionate poems wrestling with the pandemic or climate change, or her appreciation of Mahler's Ninth Symphony. She does not hold back. She follows her opening heart, and her passion for and delight in detail compels her and delights the reader.

"We come to recognize that while Mount Hunger is a real place, with a river racing down its slopes, it is also the name for our longing to find intimacy, connection, and hope."

Scudder Parker is a former preacher and Vermont State Senator and the author of the 2020 poetry book, *Safe as Lightning*. He is currently working on a second book.

FROM VERMONT GOVERNOR MADELEINE MAY KUNIN:

"Marjorie Ryerson is a thoughtful poet who finds beauty in nature and meaning in ordinary observations of daily life. The reader can find pleasure in opening up this rich collection of her work."

Madeleine Kunin served as Governor of Vermont from 1985-1991. She was the state's first female governor. She is the author of the poetry book, *Red Kite, Blue Sky* as well as the books: *Coming of Age, My Journey to the Eighties, The New Feminist Agenda, Pearls, Politics and Power: How Women Can Win and Lead,* and *Living a Political Life.*

Words of praise for *The Views From Mount Hunger*

FROM ROBERT J. RAY ("The Weekend Novelist"):

"A real hardline poet lies hidden in the poetry of M. Ryerson—landscapes ("a beach of wet toast") rivers, letters to mother ("E for the sad eyes that gave you away, A for the agonies that hid in your rooms"). The poet displays an aggressive use of white space, stacking words like a staircase in the heart, confident sallies in alliteration, repetition, precise turns of phrase, images that take root in your brain. Each poem beckons you inside, urging your eye to look deeper, take time with this line, this group of words, these studied angles of perception that narrow your focus, lines that glisten: "Heads bent like small fists against the rain.""

Robert J. Ray is the author of eight novels, including the acclaimed Matt Murdock Mystery series. He has also written several practical writing guides, including *The Weekend Novelist* and *The Weekend Novelist Rewrites a Mystery.*

The Views from
Mount Hunger

The Views from Mount Hunger

poems

Marjorie Ryerson

GReen
wriTers
press

First Printing: 2023
The Views from Mount Hunger © Marjorie Ryerson
All Rights Reserved.

Publication Date: February 14, 2023
ISBN: 979-8-9865324-9-3
Distributor: IPG / Chicago
Rights sold: All rights available.
Rights & Publicity contact: Dede Cummings dede@greenwriterspress.com

Published by
Green Writers Press
Dede Cummings
34 Miller Road
Brattleboro, VT 05301
(802) 380-1121
greenwriterspress.com
dede@greenwriterspress.com

Book design: Mason Singer / Laughing Bear Associates
Based in Montpelier, Vermont, L.B.A. has been providing graphic design and
publication expertise to clients throughout the Northeast since 1974.
(laughingbeardesign.com)

Cover and interior art: "November Ravens" © Mary Azarian
Based in Plainfield, Vermont, Mary Azarian is a woodcut artist and the Caldicott Medal
winning book illustrator of *Snowflake Bentley,* published by Houghton Mifflin Harcourt.
(maryazarian.com)

Printed on recycled paper by Bookmobile.
Based in Minneapolis, Minnesota, Bookmobile began as a design and typesetting
production house in 1982 and started offering print services in 1996. Bookmobile
is run on 100% wind- and solar-powered clean energy.

In Memory of
Krista Ragan
whose gift to all who knew her
throughout her too-brief life was
unparalleled love, kindness
and understanding.

TABLE OF CONTENTS

The Views from
Mount Hunger

The River's Wisdom

The water twists, twirls,
howling forward.
This river sucks enough water
from springs and storms
to keep plummeting its level power
beyond every next curve.

Whirlpools and eddies
—random but constant—
shiver the surfaces that spin
gold at dawn, that shimmer
blue at high noon, that
dress in tangled black silk
as the new moon ascends the ridge.

This river's wisdom
is in charge,
even during the crest of April
as snowmelt fattens
its blustering core;
even in late January,
when geometric, scored ice
seals in the current
with winter lace.

This river knows
what all rivers know.
Its language is constant music
as it breaks its glass against rocks,
thuds its drums against fallen trees,
shimmies its slick body
under dripping bridges.

This river doesn't sing
for humans who grope forward
—stopping and starting—
relying on emails,
paychecks, reality TV.

This river's wisdom is
in its *lack* of need.
This river's wisdom
is in attaining harmony
even while thundering.

This river's wisdom
is in simply being
in a place without time.

This river's wisdom is in
welcoming roots, light, eternity,
no questions asked.

This river's wisdom is
in valuing the life within.

Blending with Light

It doesn't matter the words we use.
Each poem narrates the same story.
Each poem attempts to make sense
of the jagged past, tries to walk
the thin ice of the present. Each poem
slips moist fingers into the future, snoops
into rooms whose doors are locked.

Elsewhere, biologists in antiseptic labs
bend over microscopes, hoping to
discover why words cannot move us
closer to our own parched cores.
Does it matter that scientists have
discovered the genes for risk and
uncertainty? Does it change anything

if the Big Bang never happened?
All we need to know is that when
our eyes meet those of the sun and
don't shrink away, we fuse with
the spirit of a poem. When what
we see coalesces with light—
we know ourselves at last.

Program Notes

There are more than ten
　　　　and longer than fingers

Van Cliburn
stiff on the stool
a black and white orchestra
shifting
　　　　gently behind him
black and white notes
lifting
　　　　the stillness the heart
of Rachmaninoff

Notes tumble and twirl:
　　　　　　　a river on fire
　　　　　　　thick mist on glass
　　　　　　　thudding see-saws
　　　　　　　cats' claws on skin
　　　　　　　dancers in *grand jeté*

Cadenzas pour through open summer windows:
　　　　　　　lightning on the horizon
　　　　　　　wind braiding the pines
　　　　　　　sprinting commuters late for work

Flashing fingers spin lace,
clench sunlight, breathe, mourn

Van Cliburn—
　　　　　alert grasshopper legs
　　　　　bent under the piano
　　　　　ready for the leap

If Tonight

for my daughter Emily

If tonight I heard that the bomb had dropped
and our time left was measured in hours,

I would walk to the meadow in the rain
and pick blackberries in the dark, the ripe ones

satin-soft against my fingers, sweet on my tongue,
with seeds that catch between my teeth.

I would gather the berries and bring them
back to the house to freeze for winter pies.

I would glance ahead, once more, at the photograph
of falling snow on December's calendar.

Then I would take your hand, and we would
descend the hill behind the house, and would sit

together in the tall grasses on the bank of the river
for the immeasurable time left, and be complete.

Kitty Hawk

Greengray, brownsilver
dirty pigeon-feather ocean
with fried-egg edges.
A beach of wet toast,
cupped, pocked.
Above, wings of gulls
throb like pinwheels—
bodies up up up soaring
above Kitty Hawk coast.
Hundreds of wings
with black tips, each gull
wearing two black gloves,
waving hello, hello, hello,
hello. Heads bent like
small fists against the rain.
Sudden pause, wings stop,
gull drops, engine stalls,
explosion against water.
One less fish. Hello,
hello, hello, hello.
The horizon slowly back
fuzz thin. Platinum sky.
A hair of lightning.
Tiny boat bobbing
in fog, its signal
pulsing, reflecting
in wet glass.

The Highest Wall

The highest wall
ever built
across our path
is made from
the rugged material
called grief.

When you get there:
Reach out.
Touch it.
Intimately explore
its barbed surface
with your tender fingers.

Accept its imprint
on your body.
Acknowledge
that this wall
will forever alter
your path forward.

Know that this wall
will shape new
directions for your life.
But also know
that when you
arrive at the wall,

You will find
community there.
You will never
be alone at the wall.
We are all there
with you.

Leaving Myself Behind

My car's nose draws a plumb line
on the long Delta highway that slices
the flat, arid land. Occasionally,
I pass a dollar store that promotes
its cheapness, or a solitary truck stop
that houses sleeping tractor trailers,
their motors rumbling through
the night on littered lots.

In Missouri, a boarded-over
hardware store buckles sideways
in an untilled field. In Tennessee,
a motel's once-neon "Welcome" sign
is now a faded "W"—the motel itself
long since washed away.
In Arkansas, a twisted FedEx truck
rusts on a graveyard of gravel.

Seen from my car, the Mississippi River
is a highway of swirling mud and gnarling
eddies. With intent understood only to history,
crumbling levees hide short stretches
of the proud, muscled river from view.

I am a foreigner in this place,
my Yankee accent raising eyebrows,
turning faces. I see the town of Vanleer
on the map. How do I ask how to get there?
Do I ask for Vahn-LEER? VAN-lr? Vaaan-liar?

Poverty in the heart of America
doesn't cry out. It absorbs the heat
and trudges forward, head down. The blues
aren't just a musical genre here.

In Coahoma, I mount the river's surface
in an aluminum canoe, heading south
the days and nights it will take to reach
Rosedale. The river is ropey, silver,
brown. As I begin to paddle, the river's
ancient songs tug at my arms.

Soon, the river is stretched so wide
I can barely see shore in either direction.
Brown liquid gyrates from horizon
to horizon. Even when my paddle
digs deep, the river controls my boat,
takes me where it wishes.

On this river's bucking surface,
dead trees haggle for space, boxing
each other with hollow clunks and moans.
The river's desolate shores are netted
with impenetrable walls of scrub trees.

This river sucks my body toward it
with each paddle stroke. It owns me.
And each time I stop to swim—to wash
the ovens of Mississippi summer
from my body—I shed my single layer
of clothes and slip over the gunnels
into the fierce grip of something
more than river.

As my body sinks into the fury,
I am pummeled
while my floundering limbs
learn the bliss of abandon.

I surrender to this river.
We are indistinguishable

as we wrap our fluid muscles
around each other and hold on.

In this roiling river,
I am a mere gram of shoreline dust.
I am a rootless hollow tree, bobbing the surface.
I am a brief gust of wind.
I am *water*.

The Verbs of Love

see
recognize
linger
stare

listen; inquire; explore; wonder
ache; fantasize; shiver
tingle; tremble

touch; plunge
submit; surrender

shimmer; radiate
burn; burst
melt; meld

treasure; become
breathe

stumble; struggle
cleave; weep; shut down

comprehend; compromise;
reach out; surrender; laugh

heal; bond

hold.

Vietnam 1966, and Beyond

The child curls her back,
soft and flexible as green
ferns, under the school desk
and reaches out to touch the arm
of her brother. The high-pitched
siren holds their transparent eyelids
motionless and thins their breath
into a crystal wine glass, a damp
finger circling the rim.

Thirteen Ways of Looking at Steve

after Wallace Stevens

I

The yet not-frozen stream
rushes away, rushes away,
past snow-dusted rocks,
its song in minor key.

II

Days arrive and depart
without boundaries,
blending into repetition, an intangible
dance of light and dark.

III

Thoughts of you
bring a feathered alertness
that raises its wings and soars high
over the cliff's edge.

IV

The universe has been reduced
to a poem, to thoughts of high
cheekbones under lean skin.

V

Weeks like these no longer
offer locked fingers or
two backs pressed together.

VI

I turn a piece of chocolate over
in my hands, caressing its hard form,
anticipating its softness in my mouth.

VII

My ears seek out the song
of a star's flight, high in the sky.
A white-gray film of late snow
settles on spring lawns. I haunt
the known caves of silence.

VIII

Is that the sound of a lone bagpipe,
drifting in from the far side of the mountain?

IX

Winter has buried all traces of tire tracks,
footsteps, intimations of warmth.

X

Inside has become outside, has become
nothing more than the white pines
that define the field's edge.

XI

Jackhammers overpower the solitary bagpipe.
Chainsaws warm up like swarms of bees
at the hive. The dissonance soothes.

XII

This concert has no closure.
Even the intermissions repeat endlessly,
asking forgiveness during each hiatus.

XIII

My compass stretches west.
My wings quiver and fold.

To Coleman Barks

It's like carving
into marble,
reading your poems.
I am searching
with the tools I have at hand
for the soaring eagle
trapped in the rock.

Reading your poems
is like constructing
a jigsaw puzzle of you.
I pick up a chin of a woman,
the elbow of another,
a lover's shoulder cupped
against yours,
a slip of mud beside
your crashing creek,
the many pieces of yourself
that you have gathered
at each epiphany.

In the process,
I am trying to construct
the whole of you.
Reading your poems,
I am piecing together,
carving down to
the core that is you.

It is not fully you
because it is only your words.
It is not you in the flesh
of your serious hands,
nor you in the tender fur

of your voice, nor you
in the frozen-lake moans
from the undersides
of your dreams,
nor you in the quick
frost-heaves of your eyes
when someone has hurt you.

From your poems,
I harvest your goddesses,
I gather your gourds.
Both are full of your seed.
I shake and rattle them
to learn about you,
but they only reveal
a feather of fear,
a ration of passion.

I tremble with pleasure
as I meet the crow,
the bear, the southern oak,
the poet that you are.
I, like you, have climbed
into holes left by others.
I, too, have learned
to crawl toward the light.

The W's of 2020

In isolation, we use fewer words.
We watch winter and whine.
We wash down more whiskey,
more wine. We wear winter PJs
weeks at a time. We watch
the weather while we whisper
at walls instead of wasting
our time on wacky websites.
We wonder what makes weekends
different from weekdays.
We wistfully recall work.
We wave at friends across the way
and wish we were walking
with them. We jam wet wood
into stoves, hoping to warm ourselves.
We wear out our water pipes while
washing our hands. We wander,
wrecked, through wasted days.
We wilt over worsening warnings.
We whimper. We watch.
We wait. We ask when.
We wait longer. We worry.
We grow weary. We withdraw.
We take walks. We weep.

Nightfall

Daylight disappears.
Darkness lies down beside us,
holds us in its arms.

Letter to My Mother

Tucking decades inside my belt, I look back
around curves in the path and call your name.

You are not in the trees that shelter me.
You are not in the rivers that cool my feet.

My neck cranes toward anything that moves.
My ears strain for a sound from you.

My feet want to match steps with yours.
My voice calls and calls, a bird who sings alone.

Yet still, I await your reply, your green-eyed,
sealed-and-shipped-away reply.

If I could just learn to chant the letters of your name,
I might reach the place where you are.

If I could sing the letters of your name—

    J for the jasmine of your wildflower gardens
    J for the Joshua trees in the deserts you inhabited
    J for the family jigsaw puzzle with its missing piece

If I could cry out the letters of your name—

    E for the Eros you never befriended
    E for the evenings whose veil was your comfort
    E for your sad eyes that gave you away

If I could whisper the letters of your name—

    A for the armor that shielded you
    A for the mean angles of your past and the art it inspired from you
    A for the agonies that hid in your rooms

Then I would honor the one letter that our names can't share—

N for the nightmares you comforted away
N for the navigation you taught my heart
N for the nucleus you are for me still.

The Man Who Litters School Street

I've named him Ralph, the man
who litters School Street.
I know him from the inside out.
He smokes Parliaments,
one after the other after
the other. He sips Vodka
in small airline bottles,
two bottles per block.

He crumples McDonalds' wrappers
into wads the size of a cat's head
because then they fly farther
across the green lawns.
He pitches his Coke cans high
above driveways with an inch
of soda left in them because
then the brown foam sprays
in the sunlight from the mouth hole
as the sparkly cans gyrate in air.

Ralph cruises School Street,
heaving his prized rubbish
across waiting lawns like
Nureyev doing cartwheels above
an open stage. The items spin
from his barely opened pickup
window in a perfected arch.

At home, she nags and whines;
the hall's floors are crunchy
with last winter's dried mud;
the unwashed dog barks constantly.

But out here on School Street,
Ralph's The Boss. His paper plates
spin out the truck window,
flip flopping freely in the stiff
wind, announcing freedom.

Ralph swerves his truck onto
the shoulder each time
he heaves his empty Bud Lights.
His truck slowly leaks oil
like a dream's afterthought
disturbs the waking hours.

The hue of Ralph's skin is orange,
due to all the Fritos. The truck's
exterior is rust and indigo; it's
a '94 Chevy that Ralph dragged
from a dead farmer's field.
The tires still slosh with water,
but the goddamn thing drives right.
You hear it coming; wild turkeys take
flight from the growl of the lost muffler.

There is nothing shy about Ralph.

The Lake

A sheet of dented steel, the lake
cups the sunlight in a million
bright brush strokes, tossing the light
back up toward the sun, sucking it

downward to a soft weed floor.
We skim that floor, riding the light.
We are swift fish. We are strong children,
the sap of trees in our veins.

We are waves of longing
beating our edges against the shore.
We are loopy weeds, snagging
power boats and fishing lines.

We are the weeds; we are the light;
we are the children; we are
the concrete gray surface.
We are brush strokes of light

Glistening. Glistening.

The Ideal Lover

Lives beside me, day and night.
Multiple times a day, he
gazes at me with deep love,
then gently places his forehead
against my mouth for a kiss.

In the mornings, he moans
with longing, gently pressing
against me as I awaken. He loves
to eat and is consistently grateful
for food I place before him.

He readily communicates how much
he missed me when I come home
from a few hours away. He
consistently rewards me with
gentle, affectionate love.

He quietly talks to me throughout each day,
his eyes squinting with smiles. His native
language is not mine, but I understand
everything he says. He has four legs
and a long, furry tail: my ideal lover.

Things Not to Lose

Car Key
Cell phone
Court case
Door key
Dog
Dinner
Charge card
Checkbook
Curiosity
Birth certificate
Breath
Balance
Instruction manual
Individualism
Relevance
Job
Drinking water
Awe
Love
Glove

Youth
Music
Laughter
Luggage
Hair
Underwear
Time
Teeth
Health
Hearing
Happiness
Humor
Humility
Honesty
Electricity
Ethics
Vacation
Voice
Gratitude
A healthy planet
Sensation in hands or feet

Diction
Predilection
Friends
Forests
Tennis game
Optimism
Intuition
House
Sleep
Parking space
Exercise
Knack
Nerve
Dry land
Peace
Purpose
Questions
Way
Innocence
Mind

The Solitude of November

In the meditation known as November,
branches shove thin fingers into ashen air.
The first snowflakes drift dizzily down
in slow motion, as if the clouds are
just learning their numbers, counting
out "one plus one makes five."

Naked November holds out her bare palms,
welcoming the imminent darkness to come.

In this month, lanky rivers settle heavily
into their beds, unobserved, undisturbed,
relieved to hibernate under ice until spring.
Humans are hesitant visitors to this ancient month,
a time in which Canada Geese no longer fly
and trees' last starved leaves abandon hope.

Everywhere, once-vibrant plants have folded
at their waists like tired old ladies tying their shoes.

It is best to be alone with November, a month
whose reward is ample space for breathing,
a month that follows toxic heat, brash colors,
reckless harvests, and humans struggling
to complete their summer chores—
racing against clocks that tick too quickly.

November spreads her gray silk across damp ground,
a carpet for drowsy meadows, for the few who choose to see.

It is a Pair of Soft Eyes

It is a pair of soft eyes.
It is a tongue the size of a T-bone.
It is a cow.
Not sacred, nor moon-hopping.
Not man's beast of burden, nor his ear's
bird of song. She's doubtful by the fireside
and does not fit the sleigh.
She wears no necklace of brandy.
She's just café-au-lait.
No brain of the fox, nor the
speed of a hare. No grace of
the cougar; no lynx or mink's hair.
Not used on the nickel, in anthems, on flags.
Not man, nor Mrs. O'Leary's, best friend.
Great elks in the wilderness.
Parakeets in the city. Horses
in Kentucky. Who needs a cow?
She's protein, to go with martinis.
And cow protein going out of style.
Milk full of onion grass in the spring,
and dairy going out of style.
Cholesterol. And soft eyes.
There's Coffee-Mate with fewer calories,
veggie-burgers and soymilk.
No Dior cow capes. No cops in the
Village on a warm summer night
casing MacDougal from a Hereford.
No new cars named for cows. No cows
in the zoo. No cows in the circus.
No "cow's-eye" light blue.
Daisy. Elsie. Flossie. Bessie.
Beds of mud for comfort in the
summer sun. Trees with ten-inch
shadows for huge bellies' shade.

Yellow jackets. Flies. Dried grass.
And in the end, the meat-packing house.
Soft eyes turned to cinder. Tired feet
left in the oven, not even pickled
for the market shelves with the pigs'.
Butter. Cheese. Ice cream.
Shoe leather. Soap. Glue.
500-billion McDonalds.

Instructions for the 8 Billion

A Participatory Poem

Be still and breathe in.
Pull the silky air into your abdomen.
Feel yourself fill, from your knees
to your shoulders. Shut your eyes, or
keep them halfway open.
Allow your mind to empty.
Allow your mind to still.

Be no more than the air you breathe.
Acknowledge your thoughts
as though they are strangers
passing by on the street.

On each in-breath, feel the last century
pour into you. It is your inheritance,
from flapper girls to the Korean War,
from the Model-T to moon landings,
from the parched corn fields of the '30s
to AA meetings, from New Orleans jazz
to Mister Rogers to AIDS. *All* its moments,
all its inhabitants, are alive in you.

They reside in your lungs:
    each restless commuter
    each stalled snow plow driver
    each tired biology professor in her lab,
        seeking a new cure
    each elementary school nurse, doing
        throat cultures, watching the clock.

Let them *all* float away.

Cradle your left hand in your right,
touching your index fingers
at the middle knuckle. Touch the tips
of your thumbs together and hold them still.

Continue to breathe deeply.
Slowly, silently count "one" as you breathe in.
"One" – breathe out. "Two" – breathe in.
"Two" – breathe out.
"Three." "Three." "Four." "Four."

Each breath is your legacy for this century:
    your hope for rain forests.
    your gift of lessons learned about wars.
    your anguish for the warming planet.

This present moment is all that we have.
Breathe it in. Fill your abdomen, your ribs,
with the roundness of the blue, shrouded globe,
with 14-billion-year-old stars
still traveling away from the big bang,
still a long way from wherever they are going,
stars still searching for meaning
and finding it only in the journey.

Now concentrate on your left hand.
Let the center of your being be in your left hand.
All your power, all your compassion,
all your energy is in your left hand.
Let that energy radiate to the ends of your toes
and to each follicle, where 100,000 hairs
grow from your scalp.

These breaths belong to you alone,
powerful and whole, without compromise.
This legacy is yours alone,
    in the package of your genes,
    in the wholeness of this moment,
    in your breath, in your abdomen,
    in your light.

To Anne Sexton

Anne, where are my smooth years,
my stray cats? You pull my hair,
tug my ear, turn too quickly around
the corner. A misshapen yellow
dream moves beside me,

the laboratory prize. The floor
slants forward, now backward.
I clutch my small belongings,
my birthdays like hit puppies,
my friends who sell wool.

Children who resemble you
elbow past me. I am losing
my vision, but I touch the walls.
You: the family dentist, the tennis ball
over the fence, the last hot mile

on a wet Tuesday afternoon.
You have been here all along, painting
the ceilings of small, dustless rooms,
carrying envelopes of pigtail hair,
winning an odd fame for your dying.

You words haunt me, shame me.
It is the old house I can't shake, scraps
of saved string, stamps without glue,
a broken orange egg cup, the un-sanded
edges that splinter and pierce.

Andante Comodo

Mahler's 9th Symphony, first movement

(Mahler was Austrian. The national bird of Austria is a barn swallow. It is a distinctive bird
with bright blue feathers. The cry of a barn swallow is "vitt, vitt, su-seer.")

Inside Mahler's folded chest
is a spruce branch, heavy with snow,
bowed and still, pinned against the hard
ground by its own weight. Even now,
Mahler's battered heart longs to shed
its needled burdens, longs to
empty blood from veins, to dance,
unencumbered by clothes or bones,
to transform branches into barn swallows
ascending into the sky.

Mahler bends to weave his layers
of history together into lace, hoping
to give the stories purpose at last.
He throws his rutty fingers across absent decades.
But his heart has lost its voice,
silenced by the death of his small child, by
glimmers of his own twilight in the dense
unknown. Mahler opens the doors
to the dance hall and pirouettes
toward empty stage, dragging
branches behind him. Empty chairs
line the room. Tables are folded
against the wall. The wood floors shine.
The windows glisten with rain.

Suddenly, the room is aflutter with bright
blue that uplifts effortlessly
as the anthem of *vitt-vitt, vitt-vitt su-seer,*
vitt-vitt su-seer is heard behind the rain.

Im Tempo Eines Gemächlichen Ländlers

Mahler's 9th Symphony, second movement

The tides gambol in, glide out—
elegantly bedecked dancers.

They lightly touch fingers to corseted
waists, palms to tailored shoulders.

With shoes scuffing on sandy floors,
their polished outlines twirl, pause,

bow gracefully, turn back on themselves,
and sigh. This is the timeless waltz

that intoxicates the dry land, where
impermanence rules. On sun-fevered days,

when the tides are as sluggish as ancient dogs
descending the stairs, the dancers slyly

swallow canyons, coastlines, Himalayan
peaks, marshes, icebergs, hail and mud.

And when winds stiffen or the ground
far below heaves and fractures,

those dancers toss partners from cliffs,
tear sequined gowns from bystanders huddled

against the walls. After the carnage,
the sober dancers always return, manners

intact. They bend gracefully toward each other
and link hands. The waltz resumes.

Rondo–Burleske

Mahler's 9th Symphony, third movement

Lusty winds, wanton and
selfish, recklessly flatten the pines
on the ridge. Grizzlies wail in alarm.
Meadows of wheat fold as rains breach
the fertile soil. The sky turns yellow-green.

Hurry. Hurry. Wake up. Watch out.
Disoriented deer and gray wolves
collide. Hedgehogs and lizards sprint
for shelters they cannot find.
Parrots scream. Vultures abandon
their bright meals. Wake up.
Hurry. Time is under arrest.

Small voices whimper, then
are silenced. Is anyone left
who remembers solitude or loneliness?
Can hearts still meld or splinter?
Are you listening? Do you
remember your name?

Now, as opaque mist settles
on everything, grace notes of light
comb the mist like small breaths.
The trees emit final coughs
and settle back into the wet ground,
lost and forgotten.
The mist curdles.
The light evaporates.

Molto Adagio

Mahler's 9th Symphony, fourth movement

Across the hushed crust of snow,
　　　feeble light
　　　　　sketches
pencil shadows that shudder
　　　when the wind fragments the landscape
　　　　　with its mean breaths.

The hours are like the shadows,
like the wind:
　　　irretrievable.
　　　　　We try, but cannot clutch them
　　　　　　　to our chests.

The darkness from which we flee
　　　is indistinguishable from us.
　　　　　The darkness does not ask for meaning.
　　　　　It seeks nothing.
　　　　　　　Just as grief does not judge,
　　　does not negotiate,
does not know its own name.

And when death puts out its furry palms
　　　and devours all in its path,
　　　　　our final whispers
　　　　　come
　　　　　　　from high in the throat.

We are no longer noun. We are verb—

flailing,
　　　fading,
　　　　　metamorphosing
　　into timorous laments,
into transparent memory
　　into unsuspecting geese flying north.

We are
     ephemeral echoes of moonlight
        vibrating in the wind
           just beneath the horizon,

           beyond sight

               beyond

                  sound.

Canada Geese

They head north, 60, 70 of them,
on this November doorsill to winter,
reversing the season, saturating the air
with a chorus of loose banjo strings.

When the sky is smudged chalk
to the horizon, and the snow so fine
it is no more than breath, I don't know
my way, either. Their "V" formation
is nothing more than clusters of shifting
calligraphy. Solo pilots hustle beside
an edge they hope is still there.

The geese will die young, as will many of us,
because we have all traveled more miles
per day than is healthy. My travel
is not above tree tops, but it requires
just as many take-offs and landings,
just as many meals on the run. My miles
are not map-able, but they collect tolls.
I travel miles, decades, merging into each
person I meet, moving to each town I visit.
I try to land every job, try to make music
on each instrument placed in my path.

When a bus I am riding passes through
a small Virginia town, I mentally check out
the bookstore, hire a vet for the cat,
find a mechanic, join a yoga class.

I squint down a side street. There,
through the haze, is the forest in which
I will walk, the blue of the mountain
I will climb, the white clapboards
of the house in which I will live.

I envision conversations with realtors.
I am selling my current home, packing
belongings, hiring movers,
forwarding magazine subscriptions.
I am tilling soil in my new garden,
planting bulbs, washing the new curtains,
sending out change-of-address cards.

Before my bus grinds off down the dark highway
toward the next small town, I have done
two years of work, breaking down an old life,
setting up a new one. I am exhausted.

When my cross-continental airplane
glides over a village that grips
the snowy edge of the Rockies,
I stare down at toothpick roads
from 30,000 feet, as if I will learn
their secrets. My feet twitch restlessly
under the foot rest, already
walking the snow-shrouded ridges.

When my train sails through Vancouver,
I smile at the frazzled Grand Union clerk
on the platform. I put myself in her
orange uniform. I ring up her plastic-sealed
foods. Then I visit all the bookstores
and marry, bear children with every man
who buys books beside me. I meet
all my mothers-in-law. Some husbands
leave for a year in Europe. Others go
winter camping with me in Vermont.

I sleep, pressed against hundreds
of furry ectomorphs, hairless, snoring

endomorphs. I awake to warm toes,
yearnings, mergers. I awake to unfaithfulness,
laughter, pain. My journeys are longer
than they need to be. I travel down all
forks in each road. Some of my lives
take only ten seconds to live. Some
take a week. Some take thirty years.
Some I even believe in.

I am like the geese, flying in the wrong
direction as winter bears down. My body
aims north toward the wilderness ahead.
Or else I am the one stray goose, out
of formation, wings spread, honking loudly,
seeking a home I can no longer see.

Boom

Boom
   Roar
    Crash
     Wham
       Bang
Get our attention—

but cannot come close
to the healing breath of silence,
to its calmness, its patience.

Gifts float into each of us
through the massaging fingers of silence,
through its open landscape.

Will humans ever learn
to seek out silence,
to walk its path to peace?

Will humans ever crawl
into the arms of its tranquility,
ready for its caress?

Silence is our nurturer,
caring for our hearts.
It is our essential healer.

Earth's Plea to Humans

I can't breathe; I can't breathe,
Earth cries out. Why are all
your knees pressing so hard
on my tender, aging throat?

You are blinding my sight
and lungs with smoke-dense
air, Earth weeps. Will one of you
even try to help me live again?

I am alone, without a lover
or a friend. Are you free to come
to dinner? Would you sleep
beside me in my fragile, beautiful

antique bed? Might you name
your first-born child after me?
Can you learn how to respect me?
Can you ever learn to love me?

Libretto

for Nicholas and Eliza

In the month they first opened
hearts to one another, they learned
that love comes in layers.
The top layer is the music.

The top layer is hydrogen
melded with transparent oxygen,
pouring palpably through
thirsty fingers. The top layer

is anticipation spreading willingly
like tide over rocks. It is hands
culling Chopin from the keys.
It is touch; eyes. It is sleepless peace.

In the weeks in which they each
talked alone in the darkness,
they learned that the second layer
is want; it is the precipice of the unknown.

It is the search for the familiar in
the desert of change. It is the street
without houses, a mountain
without true North. It is trust.

In the days in which they shed
expectations, in which they let go
both of asking and of needing,
they learned that love's third layer

is the in-breath. It is meadow grass
before the animals graze.
It is the pond without wind.
It is the skeletal self with flesh.

The End of the Drought

The gods' tears break loose.
Water from a fire hose
hidden in the sky
floods parched fields below,
turning the air into opaque fog.
Wave after wave of thunder
hoarsely hammers roof tops.
Streets hide under coats of
frothing brown satin.
The birch tree's leaves gyrate
in circles, like a billion pasties
glued to something
without design or gender.

Crisp grass sits passively, enduring
the assault on fragile stems.
A train howls through town,
water blinding the windows.
The greased tracks can't hold
the embankments in place. Gravel
and mud shimmy into adjacent fields.
The air is filled with the sound
of a thousand bare feet
walking through sticky mud;
the sound of twenty-million librarians
saying, "*Shhhhhhhhhhhhhhhhhh.*"

Bathtubs are emptied over the edges
of roofs. Cracked, bleached lawns
deflect churning waters that careen
forward in search of busy intersections.
Quaking dogs hide under beds.
This rage, this passion, this gift from
anemic clouds is too late for the hay crop,
too meager for depleted reservoirs.

Drivers, unable to see through
windshields, pull onto the shoulders
of roads, then climb, semi-dazed,
from their cars. They let the rain
soak their shirts, shoes, and hair,
as they turn their faces upward,

squinting like small children
walking out into the noonday sun
from a darkened movie theater.

Too soon, the pagan celebration
slows, then stills. The sky lightens.
The firemen and librarians go home.
Leaky faucets drip from the ends
of every pine needle. Drops hang
like eyelet lace along the edges
of railings, gutters, electric lines.
Open blue sky explodes onto center
stage. The streets are liquid ribbons
racing away as if late for work.

Almost Dying

Almost dying
teaches a kind of tenderness.
Almost dying
changes you
from the inside out.

Afterwards,
you walk weightless
through each remote morning,
vigilant, holding hands
with wisdom.

Almost dying
rips open a kind of hunger
that follows you
from room to room,
from shower to bed.

Each day, air
flows into lungs
that not long before
would not accept breath,
could not support life.

Now, each minute,
the fingers of your ribs
expand, contract;
reach out, pull in.
You surrender to the miracle.

Balloons of air
fill your ribs with light
from an ebony universe,
a light and a lightness

that press outward,
without limits,
from your core.

Now, with certainty,
your ribs glow
with infinite light.

Your body ebbs and flows
unselfconsciously
on the tides of breath.

The breath is real
but it does not belong to you.
It is more than substance,
more than oxygen.
Your breath is nothing—
and it is *everything*
you need.

The Dogs of Tepoztlan

In Magda's house, as night flows under the door
and the window screens breathe tepid air,
the dogs of Tepoztlan begin to bark—one calling,
calling, four answering, then another here, just
outside the door, then another five blocks away,
until a blanket of dog voices settles over the city,
barking to stop the final war, barking to stop
a plague that will destroy all food and water.

Beyond the basement screen, above my tiny bed,
feet at window level pat by, a muffled rhythm
of thin cloth shoes on cobblestones, scuffing by
in pre-dawn dampness, heading toward some dark
celebration or the 4 a.m. bus to an ill-health job
in Mexico City's Hotel Genève. In mortar holding
the gray stones of Tepoztlan's streets together,
someone has lain decorations of tiny black pebbles,
making the mortar into old-fashioned lace.
Brown and pink azalea petals blow across
the stones and collect against basement windows.

Nearby, someone is celebrating or fighting,
the resonance of guns or fireworks echoing
through the angry fog of dogs' voices.
In the back yard, Gail, the American, dressed
all in blue, feeds her pet dog. She has tied him
to the palm tree with a yellow braided rope.
She coos motherly approval as she fills his bowl
with Kibbles. Then she opens the garden door
and steps out to join the sandy dance of feet
on cobblestones. She is on her way to teach one more
day of English to children in the next valley.

Now the priest switches on the electronic speakers
in the church tower. No *Padre Nuestro* or *Ave Maria* here.

The speakers blast forth Texan country music—sharp,
nasal voices in English decrying prejudice and pain.

In this olive land, pale gringos stand out. Their six-foot
frames and blond hair highlight bank lines and bus depots.
At yesterday's fruit market, the gringo in a bright
Guatemalan shirt rubbed his shiny California energy
against a brass-dipped young mother in a pastel dress,
the man's body weight stealing oxygen from the thick air,
his hard-edged tone reflected in her mistrustful eyes.

In this valley city of southern Mexico, wastewater
is poured down the cobblestone streets by smiling
housewives. The weather is permanently overcast
from fires burning day and night. The smell of wild
roses is lost in the acrid smell of burning garbage.

Now a pig, squealing like a power saw, joins
the dog concert. A cock in the basement alleyway
announces to the smoke-soaked sky that he expects
more from dawn than this. A pig cries with the screams
of the damned, holding its throat open to mourn.
The dogs pitch their voices into a brawl—furious, rapid,
high-pitched, sharp, letting no one drown out their fury.

Small birds are now waking, their raspy throats sawing
thin planks of wood. The fireworks might as well be
bombs a few blocks away, the blasts loud enough to make
walls shake. A rusty car engine tries to turn over,
sounding like wood chips being poured down a metal chute.
The cacophony of the streets is shaking this ancient city
by the shoulders and propelling it into motion.
A loudspeaker down the hill starts an announcement:
"Uno, dos, andiamos..." but the glue of words
sinks and fades in the thick air.

Now Gail's dog sings its finger-caught-in-the-door song,
its squeaky voice a sharp wire. And now, more blasts
go off in the yard just over the brick wall draped with
white phlox and orange tulips. Royal-crown African cranes
in the yard shed their last shreds of dreams as pale color
slips imperceptibly over the tops of the hillsides.

Dona Celia calls to her granddaughter in a confetti
of broken Spanish. Later today, Baby Jesus will bring
all the jewel-eyed children of Tepoztlan out, dressed
in ironed white lace, followed by their soft-eyed parents.
This is the day chosen to honor the Baby Jesus, the day when
grown men and women carry plastic baby Jesuses the length
of the city, cradled in their arms like precious new offspring.

The plastic dolls, layered in hand-knit dresses and gold chains,
will have paper drawings of the 2,000-year-old Savior
safety-pinned to their clothes. The parade's smallest child,
her hair immaculately combed, wearing white shoes, lace socks
and a pink and white party dress, will be carried at the end
of the parade by her tiny grandmother in a faded Indian shawl.

Giraffes Don't Buy Drano

Giraffes don't buy Drano
to pour down their sinks,
then sue their towns over
poison in their tap water.
Eagles don't wander the aisles
of Walmart hunting for bargains,
their high heels squeaking
on polished floors as they smoke
packs of unfiltered Camels.
Chipmunks never send gifts
to distant cousins via 72-foot,
18-wheel FedEx trucks
that grind up Interstates
and down dirt roads,
their engines devouring
fossil fuels at 6 mpg,
their tail pipes gifting the air
with benzene, formaldehyde,
carbon monoxide, nitrogen dioxide.
Chickens don't spend money
having their feathers trimmed
or their nails painted. Butterflies
don't order toilet paper by the carton.
And when did you last see
an elephant drive his shiny Jaguar
from Dallas to Portland, or
a suited-up chimp with diamonds
in her ears fly Delta from New York
to Paris to sip Calvados and
visit the Louvre?

Harvest

At last I am shaking my own hands,
opening them to a brightly lit silence
that is nothing more, nothing less
than tranquil music.

I am finally hearing the chords
playing for me, louder than all the shoes
hurrying across China, louder than
all the BMWs in East Hampton.

I am sifting this harvest through my fingers.
It will fill me for years to come with wheat
and fruits, with clear, clean waters.

My arms gather the harvest of fears:
      —fears of stepping off
            the edges of mountains
      —fears of failed dreams,
            of restless, lonely nights
            beside troubled highways
      —fears of dying
      —fears of being alive.

My hands assemble the harvest of loss:
      —loss of parents
      —loss of children
      —loss of hope

I am culling the nutrients of my decades,
      rubbing them into my skin
      holding them under my tongue.

I wake to this music and know that intimacy
means touching fingers with those
who have shared a single measure,
      an entire symphony.

The House Windows

The house windows have been clothed in mourner's black
for more than five hours, while my four-poster bed has been
singing a love song to me, telling me how lonely it is
for the weight of my warm body pressed against its mattress.

My bed has been crooning to me:
      Don't turn on the lights.
      Don't check the time.
      Don't think about the return email you did not write
            to that long-ago friend.
      Don't consider going back downstairs to shove
            yet one more log into the wood stove.
      Don't worry that you never got all the dishes
            in the sink washed.

Come, please come, it moans. Come.
            Slide your soft body horizontally into my arms.
            Let me hold you and love you.
Shut your eyes and trust that while I hold you,
            you will forever know peace.

The bed then gets down on its knees
            and proposes marriage.
It whispers my name with a familiar timbre,
then spreads itself gently beneath me.

Migration

for Dave Grundy

(Ornithologists say that the "fee-bee" call of chickadees means "Hi, Sweetie.")

Our mouths round to fill with song.
But air rushes in, not out,
stretching our lungs to bursting.

And you, poised on the edge of the branch,
wings feathered with glistening blacks and greens,
wait
       —as you always have—
to listen.

But our mouths make only
the sound of the wind
swirling through mountain pines.

We busy ourselves,
gathering strips of straw
to strengthen our own nests.
We tip our heads left, then right,
inspecting loose chips of bark,
attending to tiny tasks at hand.

Soon, instinctively,
       simultaneously,
we all spread our wings.

The chorus of our motion grows
to a highway at rush hour
as we stretch outward while the wind
whistles through the fans of our feathers.

And still you wait peacefully, kindly,
listening silently as we hurriedly draw air
into our lungs. But our voices cannot tell you;
our throats cannot sing.

We preen our sides,
a nervous flock watching more
than a departure. A flock wanting
only to sing to you of our love.

Then, slowly, without a sound,
        your tender wings lift, stretching wide.
We recognize the moment.
We struggle. We ache. But we must accept it.

Our throats and hearts burst open
and out pours our song:
the spring song of phone wires lined
with thousands of chickadees:
        —*Fee-bee; Fee-bee; Fee-bee.*

The skies shiver with our music
as your wings begin to flutter.
Then slowly you rise and
        —accompanied by the music of our tears—
            you disappear from sight.

We will sing this song to you forever:
—*Fee-bee; Fee-bee; Fee-bee.*
        —*Fee-bee; Fee-bee; Fee-bee.*

Love Is

"Love is ice cream," the ad reads.
But no. Love is watching Tyrone Brown
dance with his bass on the stage,
while beside him, Max Roach smiles
like a new father. Love is Bach's relentless
passion, pumping across Vermont,
the radio's tiny red "on" light
the only color in the darkness, as
a pitch sky cups the frozen landscape.

Love is the details: the story
of John cradling his injured son;
the story of Beth and Bill and Whitney,
in separate, exotic countries
for one long afternoon, wanting,
above all else, each other.

Love can get sticky, when its prisms
send rainbows down ancient paths,
and its promises fail to materialize.
Love doesn't amount to much when
it comes tailor-made, ordered
from the Love Catalogue, or if it
gets cut as a deal, a *this* for a *that*.
Love isn't love if it emanates
outward without a core. Sometimes,
power or money are mistaken as love;
sometimes love is merely a safety net.

But this morning, love is belonging.
Love is the blue-papered living room
with its decades of memories.
Love is a safe place for the dog to run,
bedrooms where all our lives have slept,

a wood stove that holds its coals overnight,
book shelves where the opera summaries
are still on the top right, and the Atlases
still sit beside the poetry books.

Love is the honor we extend
to the rooms that hold us.
Love is the embracing of the fabrics,
colors, people and memories
of our own choosing. Love is a letter
from Elmore, a phone call from Wolcott.
Love is a day of warm sunlight in winter,
when we realize that we've turned
the corner toward spring, surviving
the last sub-zero morning for another season.

Hidden Treasures

Why has Kindness disappeared over the mountain ridge?
Will he ever romp back here and come to visit us again
before the sun, as is her habit, slips silently behind the barn?
And whatever happened to Honesty, who used to bring her friend,

Integrity, to dinner each day? Honesty used to beg us humans
to shed the dirty laundry from the chairs, so that she and Integrity
could each have a seat at the table. Did Caring stop in the meadow
to collect wild apples? Surely she will bring those fruits home

to share with others unwilling to reach into thorns for sweetness.
We gave Respect the right to open our mail, to hug our friends.
But somehow, humans also told him that he had to earn his
presence by doing chores and good deeds every day. He finally

shrugged and moved to the moon. The elderly Miss Faith was
kidnapped centuries ago by religion. She had kept asking humans
to trust the gray areas, even if they couldn't understand them.
When humans didn't believe that oceans lay at the end of rivers,

Miss Faith lay down and died. Trust sat by his ex-wife Hope's
bedside as she departed the world. He had written her memoir
but had never found a publisher for the book. Right before
her death, Trust used a lawyer to hijack Hope's estate.

Beauty kept writing editorials for weeklies, insisting that she
wasn't merely a physical presence but was actually inside
people's hearts, reflecting what they cared about most. She
swore her value was in meaning, not in bathing suit contests.

The twins Cooperation and Community were each individual
hands that composed classical music. The left hand was gifted.
She mastered all the notes and music's emotions. The right hand
only wanted to shake other hands and wave at the cameras.

Love—he, she, and they Love—felt overused and undervalued.
Love, the fabric of all living things, begged for understanding.
Love wanted to be the only language spoken in the world,
the one and only doctor who could keep us all healthy.

Pneumonia

I am sharply aware of the edges
of my body, just as a car-injured bird
knows her broken ribs. Penicillin
is a new invention; I am three years old.
I still don't know that for nurses with
impatient faces who sink four-inch
metal beaks of glinting hypodermics
into my buttocks, my thighs, my arms,
my back, my belly, each day,
I am merely a testing ground.

Daily, those nurses' needles rake
inflamed holes down the sides
of my body. I do not know how
disposable my body seems to them,
nor how easily they could let me
slip past the greasy grasp
of their only drug of hope.

I twist my fevered body, seeking
a few inches of unpenetrated skin
so that I can rest without constant,
searing pain. I try to not cry as I turn.
I have been taught to be brave.
In the dimly lit hospital nights,
children around me weep, whimper.
We are all lost at sea. Some are dying.
I do not yet know how easily death
buys the house down the street
and moves the furniture in.

I have no idea how this disease
saturated my tiny body. I don't know
that this same disease will become
my personal response to stress and loss
decades later. I only know that

I lie awake throughout each endless night
of an endless month, waiting for dawn,
then waiting again until the end
of each sunless day, until my father
walks into my room to visit me.

No seasons drift through open windows here,
yet wet steel music still hammers the roofs.
Somewhere in this same hospital, my mother
is stretched out on another gray bed,
though I don't know why. One afternoon,
I am suddenly loaded into a wheelchair
and rolled rapidly through hallways as
dark as sewers, pushed down dim halls,
past closed doors, up noisy elevators.

I am terrified, bewildered. Suddenly,
there she is, my mother, reaching her bony
hand toward me. I am not close enough
to touch her. Yet before my eyes can
adjust to the bright lights in her room,
invisible hands behind me jerk my chair
in a sharp half circle and roll me back out
of the room, hurrying me back to my bed
where slatted sides are snapped in place.

The boy in the bed next to mine plots
his escape for days. He repeatedly tells me
his plans. No more needles, he insists,
as I watch fear and determination twitch
the muscles of his face. One night, he makes
true his threat. After the steel-fingered
nurses have drifted away to whatever
smoking room gives them community,
the five year old beside me lowers
the side of his bed and slides his own

drug-punctured body onto the concrete floor.
When he is gone, I miss him.

I think his name is David, but I'm not even
sure. His escape plans were the only drama
in this room, each day, besides the constant
presence of pain. In his absence, I watch
the hands of the clock, minute by minute,
shake their way from 2:10 a.m. to 4:15 a.m.

Suddenly, two fierce men in white silently
carry my young friend's limp body back
into our room and dump it unceremoniously
into the cold bed beside mine. They raise
the sides of David's bed like the walls
of a jail around his unconscious form.

I shrink in silence, fearing my knowledge
of his escape will bring to my own aching body
the same drug that has turned his defiance
into limp, unconscious compliance.
The two male nurses strap David's thin arms
to the side rails of his bed, and walk out of
the room. I lie very still, trying to breathe
silently and to not cough. I suck in my own
pain, and stare. Will David ever wake up?

As days go by, the nurses make sure their needles
keep David silent and unmoving. No father comes
to see him each night. My father's daily visits
are the reason I hang on. He is the reason I endure.
He radiates the outside world from his clothes,
the bustle of a city work life, the anxiousness
of a caring father. My father is all smiles,
but then, in what feels like seconds,
he is gone again until the next night at 6:00.

Chic Chick

Black crepe to mid-calf.
Heels. Nylons. Pearls.
Soft eye makeup.
Napkin on lap.
Hands folded.
Neck long.
Lipstick.
Blush.
Sushi.
Silence.
Nodding.
Could be love.
Things not said.
Could be money.
No one's taking notes.
No one's spilling the beans.

Mornings

Mornings are like fingerprints: no two are the same.
In July, the sun crests the tall pines by 6 a.m.,
burning mist off the lush grass, transforming
the town's already grinding backhoes into gold.
Wide mouthfuls of angora clouds rest against the sky.

As the season dips into early fall,
the 6 a.m. sun is only midway up the pines,
sending laser beams through the branches,
highlighting the edges of leaves tipped orange and rust.
The light shines through white pine needles, turning
them into dancing silver pins, stitched to black arms,
glittering as if they might never dance again.

By November, the dawn landscape fades, darkens.
The fields are luminous with fallen leaves.
It isn't long before the 6 a.m. walk with the dog
is in total darkness. A sliver of moon
illuminates the frozen brown leaves underfoot.

On this particular November morning,
the sky is a flat, oil-refinery gray.
White woodwork on the red barn glows
from a streetlight somewhere down the road.
Stars are surprisingly bright, in this hour
of the wolf, as they scatter bright abundance
across the rim of the ancient sky.

A cold front predicted, a bank of clouds
has edged the western mountains.
As if on cue, a long, white gash opens,
slicing the cloud bank in half—an
ominous smile the size of New England.
It seems to say: *Keep walking away.*
It seems to say: *Be silent. Watch underfoot.*
        Hard times are coming.

New Math

My body twists like ocean currents
against your unfurled, loosened
mainsail-in-a-windstorm body,
creating a new body—our body.

This new body, which is more
familiar than my own, bakes
in the oven of our immense bed.
It ruts the soft mattress, nesting,

lusting, defining a sense of home.
It shoves a leg off this side, drops
an unguarded shoulder off that.
It melds, congeals, shifts constantly

through the night, voraciously
seeking its own silky-skinned bliss.
The slow-gyrating mass of our body's
ambrosia fills the shorelines

that jut from necks and lips.
It slips into welcoming gullies
of elbows, ankles and legs.
It unhesitantly floods the oceans

and rivers of the new landscape
we have created. Our body stays
half awake throughout each night
to relish the pleasure of liquid limbs

against liquid limbs, of torsos fusing.
Our body melts and repositions itself
throughout the hours of night, secretly
dreading the blithe light of dawn.

Venice

In Venice, the fever holds in you, your sleepless
alphabets tucked in its glittering envelope.

While you twist the sheets of our cheap hotel,
I walk the streets, avoiding all museums:
the Ca Doro, the Academia, pink-feathered churches
collect entrance fees, moonlight, the unaligned and angry waters.

I trace the swirling cobblestones back through narrow streets.
At small round tables on the canal's edge, the espresso
is like steamed bark and the ocean-going ships loll by
like semis lost in a dream.

Outside the Biennale, two old men fish for garbage with strings.

The gray and purple weather wraps me, spins me.
Iridescent air from mainland factories drops its loam
on loosely-jointed pigeons from St. Mark's.

Venice: twists of lemon in relief; sand-blind beauty:
        Young boys in shorts beating with
                sticks at a cat caught in a fence.
        The watermelon man, a pure, gemmated Norman Mailer;
                a genial, gate-legged George C. Scott,
                        chest deep in the plumb-ripe melons in his boat.
        A statue to those lost at sea, wet female body splayed
                flat along a pier, stone draperies fluted high
                around her head; two stone feet, each 18" long,
                suspended in air; the waves from the canal sifting
                over her form. Green algae eating her face.
        Scraggy back canals, the boats and window widows
                thick as laundry on second story ropes.
        Tourists in white shoes with Italian dictionaries.
                Tourists in clogs reading Frommer.

Two scrubbed old flower men: fresh chrysanthemums,
   gladioli, scorched blue carnations; chewed-lace
   flower shadows pitched thirty feet by the five o'clock sun.
Curving airless streets pinched by chipped porcelain buildings.
A child dancing by herself, eyes shut, head bent sideways
         almost touching her shoulder; dress of spattered flowers
         twisted high, small white hands bent stiffly back
         from the wrists.
A cafe where, in the slender dawn, a young man drops
         the poles of umbrellas, closed in on themselves like
         hemlocks, into slick silver holes in the tables.
One by one he spins the trunks and the blue, the green folds
         swing in ripples, opening wider and wider,
         spinning upward until a full circle has formed and
         the pleats are stretched taut against slim steel arms.
               The cafe is open.

Where Streetlights Don't Erase the Stars

It isn't fame I crave, or money.
It isn't more hours in the day.
My craving is set high in rugged mountains
where, in January, snow pitches sideways
against the pines and piles eight feet up
the front door. In this place, in summer,
rain clouds sculpt massive black quilts
above the ridges, while needles of lightning
dance in the northwest. Summer also
brings sun so bright it liquefies
back muscles and is like cut glass
against our eyes. Summer brings nights of
crickets symphonies in the meadow
or the taffeta skirts of rain on the roof.

In this place where I imagine I live, I move
lightly through my irregularly-shaped,
open house, with its large windows
facing in four directions. The house
sits in a high meadow of grasslands full
of wildflowers, birds, clusters of birch trees.

The back of the house is pressed against
boulders that shove their elbows out
from the land. The front of the house
faces sharp-ridged mountains where
12,000-foot peaks cast families of shadows.
I do yoga while taking in that view.
The hawks and eagles are my blood sisters.

My body is healthy. No matter
how many years I have lived, my muscles
are taffy young. Nothing hurts in any limb.
All the core wiring works.
I own no fast cars, and need no fancy tires.

An old pickup is parked near the house.
I use it for lumber, groceries.
I wear sweaters, pants, boots every day.
A wool jacket is never far from me,
as the wind tickles, then shakes the walls.
My hair is short and wind-swept;
my eyes 20-20. I am at my computer,
writing. Or I am painting the view or
photographing tiny details that draw me in.

In the cooler corner of the living room
sits the grand piano inherited from my father.
Lamps sit on dark wood tables. At twilight.
I walk from room to room, turning on the lamps.
Their light glows back from the wood walls
and reflects against glass windows.
As I turn on the lights, the inside of the rooms
suddenly become the fulcrum for all of life.
The house's windows wait for tomorrow's dawn,
when I will again be outside again, walking with
my dog, absorbing the mountains, tasting the sky.

Perhaps a partner shares the house with me.
If he is here, he is someone with kind eyes.
He is quiet around the edges, but funny,
creative, bright of mind and eye, a good cook,
a wise companion, an intense and constant lover.
If he isn't in the house while I'm writing,
he is off in the woods watching birds,
writing notes; gathering greens.
When we are together, it is just the two of us:
it is me, as I know myself now. It is him.
His hands are my doctor; they mend me.
My mouth is his therapist; it heals him.
He joins me in yoga each dawn. We stretch

our bodies together in a rhythm and knowledge
that confirms a union far deeper than words.
In winters, I bend to rebuild the fire
in the living room stove. Glowing coals
greet me from the morning's blaze.
In winter evenings, I walk to the far,
quiet end of the house, where I build
a fire in the bedroom fireplace. It will
heat the feather comforter and wool
blankets, as well as the satin sheets below.

Tomorrow will bring a warm enough afternoon
to sit by the stream that runs wildly over
its same rocks most months of the year.
We hear it from the bedroom at night,
a white noise burbling a lullaby as sweet as
any mother has sung, comforting us as
we hold each other through the night.

Our house has a small garden, though
it is barely weeded. The garden contributes
lettuce, potatoes, vegetables, herbs and flowers
until frost. A greenhouse inside the kitchen
opens to the south, a glass chapel that
fills the house with the moist smells of
fresh earth, basil, lavender and mint.

In the kitchen, the wood stove's bright face
glitters at us through blizzards and through
the frozen-ground November before snow has
sealed us in. Birds congregate busily at the feeder
I have hung outside the kitchen window.

This is a land without leash laws. My dog
runs the woods trails with me each morning,

and lies behind me in my study, later, as I write.
This place, this life, is something like the life
I have already, but then not like it at all,
because here, I am always at peace.

We play music with our bodies, with our
fingers, with our minds. Other music plays here,
too. Our stereo tiptoes into our ears through part
of each day, or paints the walls with sound,
whether it is Chet Baker or Mahler we want
rattling our bones. Other times, we lie
together in the darkness, listening
to each note of a breathless cello concerto.

Outside, in fall, long grasses blow—
brown, green, gray, shifting daily in
shade and hue, like the sky. We listen
to weather reports on the radio.
We peer at huge stars from the deck's
telescope at night, or lie back on deck chairs,
wrapped in quilts, watching shooting stars.

I am an intimate companion with the shapes
of the fields around the house, with the location
of each tree, with the sun's trajectory from
July to June. I can tell the exact outdoor
temperature without a thermometer.
There is never a day I am not outside.
I ski through the woods, snowshoe
to the summits, hike the 10 miles
to town when the roads aren't plowed.

The air here is clean, free of pollutants,
free of industrial garbage. I live
west of the Mississippi, north of Kansas,

west of Iowa, north of Denver.
Perhaps I am living on the western slopes
of the Cascades. But perhaps, too, I have
never left Vermont. Perhaps I have
merely fled village life and retreated
to the soft, quiet flesh of Vermont's
Greens Mountains. The only thing
of which I am sure is that in this
four-season corner of time,
I am looking out only
in the directions I choose to see.

This house is filled with books:
books written by friends who send me
their latest published works,
books inscribed with love.
There is always enough time to read.
I spend hours in my darkroom, making prints.
I spend every early morning, after my walk
with the dog, in my office, writing about
the details of this uncompromising paradise,
editing other people's books, sending out
poems to be published by the *Kenyon Review,*
Plowshares, the *New Yorker, APR.*

Every so often, we host a gathering
of a dozen or so bright, shaggy friends:
artists, writers, musicians, aging newsmen
with graying hair, sun-dried faces, easy smiles,
crow's-feet eyes. We talk about the news,
about creativity, about mind-body
connections, about conflicting theories
of time. We lean back into the sofas
and put our feet on the furniture.

Every morning, I wake rested.
I move through each day like
a rayon curtain in the breeze, fluid,
flowing, the light glistening
off my edges and shining through.

Recipe for 2021 Pain Muffins

Mix together:
>Five pounds of sadness
>Three tablespoons of collapsed vertebrae
>Two cups of shoulder surgery gone awry
>A close friend with terminal cancer
>Twenty teeth-gritting muscle spasms
>Thirty un-repairable life crises
>Half a quart of un-diagnosable illnesses
>100 overdue bills
>Life lived with no clear future
>60,000 murders of innocent people
>And a global pandemic.

Once blended:
>Combine resulting sauce with
>9,000 gallons of excess CO_2
>One 90-mile floating island of plastic
>and the water from 200 melted icebergs.

Stir for sixty seconds with sharp knife blade:
>Put mix into muffin pans.
>Don't turn on oven. The Earth is hot enough.
>All muffins will bake instantly.
>Eat all the muffins.
>Walk in circles for 12 months.

Reach Out

A loving dog walking by us, a wave
through our closed bank window
are pandemic survival tools. Emails
with long-ago friends in Larchmont
or Oxford help, as well. As do walks
down familiar, abandoned streets
of our towns, even at 30-below zero.
Keeping us going are small tasks
that we do for others rather than
for ourselves. In '20-'21, we quickly
learn that our spirits need more
than simply doing the laundry.
The pandemic has taught us that if
we help our sagging porch roof
by shoveling the two feet of snow
from it, the roof will be grateful,
even if it can't say so. And the roof
will reward us, in return. So thank
the roof. Thank the librarian for
the book you recently borrowed.
Thank the supermarket cashier
for ringing up the cat food
you are buying. Thank the staff
at the landfill for accepting
your trash. And always thank
yourself for holding on.

Reach out.

How to Write a Poem that is Brief

Pick a topic like describing a leaf.
Don't attempt to write a poem about grief.

Avoid any poems describing a thief.
While you're at it, skip having a motif.

And be sure to stay away from comic relief
or poems about the Great Barrier Reef.

Instead, write a poem about corned beef.
Or else craft a poem about a handkerchief.

And don't dare show your finished piece
to your favorite editor-in-chief.

Body/Mind

Every day, Body, the obedient sixth grader, does exactly what
she is told. She sits up straight, follows all directions. She stays quiet
while teacher talks, always keeps her iPad near. She gets her homework
done on time, her science essays polished, her fractions correct,
her skill-builder words memorized, her chocolate desserts shared.

Mind is the benevolent dictator in Body's life. He oversees her
from his throne, raises his voice sternly if he is displeased, keeps
support staff on alert, orders the $200 Merlot. Mind knows how
to dip gray neurons into the waters of curiosity and how to flip quickly
through the morning news. If Mind wants to be entertained,

he orders a rocket to the moon. He flies first class. He insists
on the detour to Mars. Meanwhile, Body keeps her sugar intake low.
She gets A's in French class. She gets eight hours of sleep
each night and wears clean undies. She never forgets her veggies.
Teacher insists that Body obey Mind's commands.

But today, Body's front row seat is empty. Is she ill?
Body wouldn't play hooky. But neighbors saw Body flee
the back door and ascend the mountain behind the school.
She was wearing pink corduroys and no shirt, her legs and torso
dancing. Mind is called on the hot line. He calls in the Law.

Law orders Body back to school, insisting she obey her
P's and Q's, that she salute the flag. But Body only dashes
farther up the mountain. She sings with the birds. Her grin
melts nearby snowfields and shines light into the valleys.
It looks like Body is growing wings? How can this be?

Is that Body who now hollers through a bullhorn, announcing
to the world that she is in love; that she alone rules?
Could it be that Body is now shredding her lifetime contract
with Mind, letting the paper contract float away—carried
by the soft winds that reliably wipe the mountains clean?

"A table, a chair, a bowl of fruit and a violin;
what else does a man need to be happy?"
-Albert Einstein

Six Adagios

Shostakovich's 15th string quartet

1. Elegy

A reclusive hand reaches, without haste,
through the shafts of light ahead,
light that pleats the hollows between
the forest's tall pines. The hand stretches
away rather than toward. It is lonely
but it seeks nothing.

The hand gradually separates into two hands
clasped together, still reaching.
The hands settle on dank moss.
The moss folds around them, shadowing
them in darkness. The hands pour
loss and tenderness from their palms.

2. Serenade

My hands close on your tousled hair,
moments after anxiety has thrown its shawl
over your eyes. As I sit, barely breathing,
holding death between my palms,
I imagine a spring stream pouring
through me, as it did below me,
that fall, when you and I had walked
in twilight through the woods you loved.

Deafened by the water, you had
dropped down to sit on a boulder
at the crown of the falls. As I walked on,
my legs suddenly weakened.

At the fall's crest, my feet slid
through wet leaves. Beneath me,
a crevasse plummeted down thirty feet
to boulders and the angry falls below.

In anguished slow motion,
I pitched my body sideways
to save my own life. As I sank
to the ground, the river below changed
from dragon to human to water.
Smiling, you rose and came toward me,
oblivious. You reached for my hand,
intending to lead me back toward
my car and my own life.

3. Intermezzo

Goodbye to penguins. Goodbye to krill.
Goodbye to Arctic ice. Goodbye to falcons,
snowy owls, science, and homes on the beach.
Goodbye to the Grand Canyon and to
the ozone layer. Goodbye to buttercups
and cuckoos and heirloom seeds.

What is left? Is it chocolate cake?
Is it violence? Is it pretense? Is it two crows,
atop two pines, talking through
the length of a Friday afternoon?

4. Nocturne

I watch you sleep, your face relaxed,
your mouth at peace. You are so beautiful
that I cannot sleep. The crows outside the window
still chatter from the tops of the pines.

5. Funeral March

The morning windows glisten with your absence.
The spoons in the drawer are unused.
The tea box is unopened; the sheets smooth.

My hand reaches through the rays
of light, but fails to find its pair.
The silence has sucked the solar system dry.

6. Epilogue

Light slices me from the inside out
as I wake with a start to unrecognizable
noises in the street below.

Darkness

We have a choice
between types of darkness:
the darkness that obscures
or the darkness of inner peace;
the darkness of loneliness
or the dark comfort of
one's lover on a winter's night;
the darkness that haunts
long hallways, or
the darkness that asks us
to prepare a longer table.
There is the darkness of barren
land, but the darkness
of moist earth in spring
is our sweetest reward.

My Father's Essence

In his death, my father poured
his essence into my hungry arms.
I shimmer with him.

Now, I drive the rain-weary highways
for us both, and sleep
on the edge of death
so that he knows comfort.

I spend my most tender moments alone
so that his presence isn't hammered
by strangers he is unable to love.

I take him to the edges of rivers
where we sit, listening,
no longer sealed by boundaries
of skin and emotion.

The river pours into us both
and my father holds out his hands
like a child in a rainstorm,
accepting water as the supreme sensation.

My father is in my ears, gathering
symphonies and string quartets.
My father is in my handshakes
when honors flower for us both.

He is the silk of the sea
as I skinny dip at dawn.
He is flannel love in winter.
He is headlights on the dark road.

Poems

Poems are the scraping away of the surfaces
to get at what is underneath. Poems are
the last-gas-before-desert hope for us.
The words clarify. The words deceive.
Thoughts constrict to fit the shape
and length of lines. Experiences
are simplified to fit the page.
Contradictions are edited out,
and the hope for the shape of the future
picks up its carving tools and reworks
the past that has tumbled out
through the open mouths of the fingers.

Turning of the Season

Oh, this bright wind,
it pierces the ebony sky
with pin pricks of stars
yet brings a night so black
I can only hear the tree branches
thrashing on the fourth floors
of the sky, their leaves
crashing together
in the moist-grass darkness
like impotent armies
battling to the death.

It is late August.
Although fall hasn't yet
made her flashy,
street-walker entrance,
tonight, summer has run away,
clutching her long, flowered
skirts—cold, hungry,
unaccustomed to loss,
afraid of the dark.

My dog is as black as the night.
He is wild tonight,
his eyes mistrusting
everything. He strains
to see the demons
who have woven their hands
through the tangled hair
of his wind-blown tail.

He yanks his leash toward
the safety of our house's
back door, and I, my heart
in a place too deep to remember,

resist, pulling him out
toward the empty clutches
of the backyard
where it is so dark,
I cannot even see my dog
or the hulk of my big barn.

Suddenly, I feel
my dog's weight shift.

Now, he strains hard
toward the night.
What is he doing?
Why is the leash
suddenly slack?
Am I alone?

I am in a reoccurring childhood dream:

> *The train is barreling toward me, 90 yards away.*
> *I am frozen to the tracks, watching its power*
> *bear down on me, hearing the whistle of alarm,*
> *knowing that adults on the platform watch in horror,*
> *aware that I cannot move from the train's path.*

Visual Histories

Deep snow tells the story
of its visitors. In early morning,
deer tracks link fingers with
drunken dog prints across village
yards, while knife-blade slices
are carved in lawns from icicles
that have fallen from gutters above,
leaving necklaces of diamonds
in straight lines around houses.

Tiny, double-ring circles, scattered
randomly on the top of the snow, are
so shallow they clearly must be
the residue of visits from snow fairies.
Other deeper holes across yards
suggest that the 20-pound monk—
who shows up after each snowfall—
returned again last night, pacing
while meditating: slowly
breathing in, breathing out.

Scattered tiny gray holes
in frozen snow beside roadways,
illustrate how many cars have
splashed their way through
the highway's salt-melt.
Just behind those dirty dots are
concrete-stiff, sand-grayed piles
that town plows have sculpted
in recent storms. Curving ski tracks
and winding snowmobile paths
behind those piles convey
wild joy rides by recent guests.

Beside one driveway, cat prints
tell just how far one pet traveled
before deciding it was too cold
underfoot. The tight half circle
his paws drew, at the end of
the straight line his feet had sketched
in fresh snow, tells just how
quickly he changed his mind,
fleeing back through his cat door
into his dry, warm home.

Some Men Kiss

Some men kiss like backhoes
preparing the back yard
for the swimming pool.

Others kiss like sparrows clinging
to the telephone lines, their claws
gripping the wire, hanging on
for dear, dear life.

Some kiss like Harleys
blasting over the terrain, spraying
dust that obliterates the sun
and burns the eyes.

Some kiss like children
kneeling beside their beds,
thanking God for Mommy and Daddy.

Some kiss like math,
the chapter on tangents
followed by the chapter
on integral equations,
expecting all formulas to balance
in the end, and the answers
to be either right or wrong,
expecting to earn straight As.

Some kiss like moths
on a screen door, their
dusty wings pinging
the rusty metal
in an involuntary dance
with death.

Some kiss like toothbrushes,
inspired to clean each crack,
massage every gum.

Some kiss like vultures
working the carcass of the deer,
snipping with sharp nibbles
on soft, available flesh.

Some kiss like a long sleep
after a drunken night out with the boys,
settling their bodies down heavily,
losing consciousness, their lips
bench-pressing 500 pounds.

Some kiss like super-glue
mending shards of a broken vase,
the glue stronger than the vase,
a glue to last 10,000 years.

Some kiss with tongues of
river-bottoms, some kiss with
tongues hard as studded tires
in January, some with jackhammer
tongues, urgently broadcasting
Morse Code.

Long Miles

Because she put him there, in the hollow
between her breasts, where her heart floated
too near the surface

Because she held him there while he cried
his bent past, loved him there while he
churned fear and hate into shapes,
trusted him there

Because she drove long miles away
only to still need him

Because she loved the view from the kitchen,
she bought the house built on the toxic waste dump
and moved the furniture in even though pipes and barrels
were still visible, poking out from the front lawn

Because she opened the dusty shutters
and let in the storm, and waited
for the light to clear the clouds

Because she could never adequately close
the shutters, though her feet stormed away and
her mouth suffered thousands of casualties in the battles

Because she folded up the sheets
and hung the winter chains in the empty barn
a barn that tilted to one side
with a leaking roof and a crumbling foundation

Because time doesn't heal all wounds
it just seals them

Because she did not discriminate
about what she let into that hollow
space between her breasts

She chained herself in the barn and watched
the rain drip down in whirlpools around her
while she wrote songs about tiny pebbles
on the stream's bottom: how they glisten in the sun.

Letting Go

A flood, a fire, a tornado,
moving away, downsizing.
Throughout our lives, each
of us repeatedly faces our
possessions and is forced
to admit their uselessness.

It might be the antique chest
we inherited, the photographs
we took as a child, the striped
umbrella from Brazil. Each
item eventually blends memory
into function, purchase into
purpose, all eventually
becoming excess weight.

In our final minutes of life,
it is the daughter's eyes brimming
with love and the agony of loss,
the son's gentle, deep voice,
that are the only possessions
worth anything. And even
those are transitory.

Night's Breath

I wonder if night's breath plays
its flute to the stream, inspiring dreams
in sleeping fish. Or if the stream
stretches its sparkling fingers
around miles of its own violin
while night above leans heavily down,
pulling the bed covers over its head.

I wonder if the dying cedars
lining the stream banks
bend toward their gyrating,
reflected images. Or instead,
if the water dances upward
toward starved tree roots,
offering its song as
nourishment as well as hope.

I wonder if the percussions of time
ask the vibrations of instant gratification
to dance, while the stream plays
its piano and sheds tears, or if the
vibrations challenge the percussions
to determine who is stronger,
wiser, kinder, more enduring.

I wonder if the fireflies see anything
but themselves conquering the dark,
and if they assume the powdered sugar
of stars above is merely their own
reflection illuminating another
night, as it seeps in above
distant mountain ridges.

Ask My Hands

Ask my hands anything. They can
tell you who I was at age eight.
They can recount for you rhythmic
pleasures they have stored as bird cries,
memories they have archived
of ravaged landscapes under siege.

Ask my hands what they know of you
and they will reach out to close the distance
between us. They will paint on your landscape
a map where they travel the back roads, stopping
here for coffee, there to photograph the view.

My hands will talk to you through
the thin layers of skin between us,
drinking in your stories, meeting
your mother, dancing with you and
your honey at the junior-high prom.

Tell my hands everything. Give away
the contents of the bottom drawers.
Rip open your beauty and let the dust motes
rise. While our words stumble over what
our bodies already know, your hands
can glide me safely through harbors
where sailors have drowned. My hands
can nimbly step into the orchestra pit and
take up the cello while you start to conduct.

Is it hard to admit how much our hands know?
Let them bless our fugitive flesh.
Let them teach us to open to this quietude,
where meaning is measured without words.

Music Doctors

The world unravels, burns and
shreds in ways none of us have
imagined and in ways none of us
knows how to repair. Yet
healing tears flood our cheeks
as Bach's BWV 974 Adagio
saturates the room. Massenet's
"Meditation" Adagio also raises
the rivers of our souls' gardens,
as does Arvo Pärt's *Spiegel im Spiegel*.
Music doctors are as old as
the human race. These healers
drench us with the only medicine
that truly cures, medicine that numbs
our agony so that we can go on.

Acknowledgements

"To Anne Sexton" was previously published by the *Carolina Quarterly*

"Rondo – Burleske" was previously published in the book *Music in the Air*, released in 2013 by Outrider Press

"The Highest Wall," was published in the *World Bank Quarterly*, October 2021

"Music Doctors" was published in the *World Bank Quarterly*, June 2022

"The Lake" was published in *Vermont Almanac*, November 2022

Marjorie Ryerson is an award-winning book author, journalist, photographer, teacher, and poet. From 1991 until 2005, she served as a tenured full professor of journalism and photography for Castleton State College. While teaching there, she won the best new teacher award, and, ten years later, she was awarded the Faculty Fellow award for the entire Vermont State College system. For over 20 years, Marjorie has taught poetry for Middlebury College at the New England Young Writers Conference at Bread Loaf. Prior to teaching, she was the editor of the *Times Argus'* weekly magazine, *Country Courier,* followed by serving as features editor for the *Burlington Free Press*. Marjorie also served as a First Wednesdays' lecturer for the Vermont Humanities Council, sharing with Vermonters her experiences gained while writing her 2005 book *Companions for the Passage: Stories of the Intimate Privilege of Accompanying the Dying.* Marjorie's 2003 art photography book *Water Music* won both national and international recognition and awards, and she then ran the Water Music Project (www.water-music.org), which grew out of the publication of that book. From 2010-2016, Marjorie served as a member of the Randolph Selectboard and, from 2013-2017, as Vermont State Representative for the Orange-Washington-Addison district. Marjorie has a graduate degree in poetry from the Writers' Workshop at the University of Iowa.